I0173130

Musings on Life: For Those Who Think, Feel and Wonder

A collection of original quotes
by Bruce Marshall Sterling

Stage 3 Press
Boulder, Colorado

Musings on Life:
For Those Who Think, Feel and Wonder

Copyright @ 2023 Bruce Sterling
All rights reserved. No parts of this book
may be reproduced or used in any manner
without written permission of the
copyright owner except for the use of
quotations embedded in articles or
reviews.

BruceSterlingLLC.com
Stage 3 Press
Boulder, CO

First paperback edition 2023
ISBN 978-1-7365611-2-6 (paperback)

Dedication

I dedicate this book to all my teachers, friends and family that have helped me discover so much of the physical world of nature and society, and the inner world of our psyche, spirit or whatever word may fit your vocabulary and spiritual orientation. Some of the unnamed people to whom I dedicate this book had to suffer through my slow growth and stubbornness. I apologize for my stubbornness, not so much my slow rate of progress. We grow at our own rate. Still, there were regrettable consequences.

I especially want to posthumously extend my gratitude to my editor and friend, Madeline Goldstein, whose inspiration and support for this project helped move it along to completion. She conveyed over and again, "less is more." In contrast to my rebellious nature, as well as paying homage to her words, I agree, "more or less".

Table of Contents

Preface

This book came about as a result of a lifetime of observation, trainings, coaching and the desire to share what I've said with a larger audience.

Life is curious enough. The origin, the purpose and the magnificence of the place in which we reside is beyond comprehension. Throw people into the mix and it gets more beautiful and bizarre.

The world with people holds tremendous love, joy, kindness, compassion as well as unimaginable fear, cruelty and greed. It's all so strange to live in this world. It's also challenging and inspiring to eke out sanity, promote well-being, create institutions that benefit others and to grow into our more refined selves. Overall, it's not a bad place to be for the short time we get to visit before moving back into the unknown, potentially of indescribable love and beauty or nothingness. I don't know but since I'm making up a story, I prefer one that inspires me.

Part One

Irony of life

+++

Methinks the tower of Babel
was not just of words
but thoughts as well;
and thus irony began.

+++

It is our destiny to be
who we are.

+++

We have to learn
through the constraints of our personality.

+++

I spent
half my life hiding;
the other half trying to find me.

+++

Shattered glass
makes the kaleidoscope more interesting.

+++

I made
so many wrong turns
I ended up in the right place.

+++

Sometimes I'm amazing;
sometimes I'm just a maze.

+++

What if
I was the person I wanted to be all this time?

+++

If I would have realized
how much fun
it would be
to be me
I would have started a long time ago.

+++

If life is so funny
you want to be in on the joke.

+++

The only one who's been in a tizzy about you
is you.

+++

I don't know God's first or last name
but surely
Irony must be
the middle name.

+++

Irony
is God's sense of humor,
but does it have to be so pervasive?

+++

Sometimes
irony warms my heart,
especially when it's set to steam.

+++

It's tough being human
and being yourself.

+++

Humanity
is inherently flawed.
That, in and of itself, is disappointing,
but the way we've manifested it
is even more insane.

+++

We're living a reality show.

+++

You can't see your privilege
if you're attached to your story.

+++

Wise-wise;
why's make you wise.

+++

The antithesis of insanity is creativity.

+++

You can be held captive by what you seek
or freed through what you create.

+++

We have personal responsibility
not to be misguided
by mob mentality.

+++

You can't
piss on your yard
and expect roses to grow.

+++

Humility lessons
don't have to be humiliating.

+++

Life teaches us
to let go of life,
one attachment at a time.

+++

Even when
you stand in your light,
you'll cast a shadow,
unless the light comes from above.

+++

Everything is obvious
once it's revealed.

+++

Life is so odd;
a miracle
yet with a curious purpose,
if any.

+++

Life is about
trying to figure out
what life is about.

+++

It's hard
to fit life
into a lifetime.

+++

Live
like your life depends on it.

Love that way too.

+++

How much do I **have** to give and
how much do I **have to** give?

Very different questions.

+++

Life
is a subjective experience
that dwells within objective structures
like time, space and organizations.

+++

Life continues
to be an unknown at every step.

+++

The trick is
to awaken within the dream
and still be yourself.

+++

Defensiveness
is a way to avoid shame.

+++

Is "an addictive personality"
code-word for
"I have unresolved trauma?"

+++

I've been told
I think too much.
I'm not sure that's true.
I'm just trying to make sense of the world,
but it still seems pretty crazy.

+++

Perhaps the things we lost along the way
were actually payments
for lessons we learned in the process.

+++

Wisdom of life

~~~

Wonder vs religion:
the difference between awe and theory.

One is living it,
the other is talking about it.

~~~

Idle time is my time;
unstructured, free time,
the fleeting eternity.

I pause and relish in the moment.

~~~

You spend both money and time.
You can earn more money if you want
but there's no way to earn more time.

Use time for what you truly value.

~~~

The intervals of life
from inaction to action
can drag on endlessly
or flash like magician's paper.

~~~

We're all in the dying process.
Some of us will just get there sooner.

~~~

Things take a long time to happen so fast.

~~~

Looking backward is invaluable when it teaches
you how to walk forward.

~~~

Knowing the right thing makes you smart.
Doing the right thing makes you wise.

~~~

You can't get past ignorance
if you keep ignoring what you've done.

~~~

You can give attention or
you can pay attention.

~~~

You live out your patterns
until you change your self-worth.

~~~

Shadow work
is invaluable.
It turns on your light.

~~~

To live and learn,
follow your love.

~~~

Lessons and insights
are available throughout your life
if you look
with an open mind and soft heart.

~~~

Everybody's got to be somebody
so you may as well be yourself.

~~~

I used to be scared of the dark
because of people that hide in the shadows.

Now I'm scared of people
that hide in **their own** dark shadows.

~~~

My motto:
Do what others don't or won't.

~~~

Self-healing
is the only healing.
Self-love,
the most important love.

~~~

Sharing self-love
is what we often call love.

~~~

Knowing what something isn't
points to what it is.

~~~

I'm going for the "fountain of use."
Use yourself fully and
it'll feel like a worthwhile life.

~~~

Time is **the** commodity of life.

Deepen and expand each moment.

You won't get more time,
but you'll get more quality time.

~~~

The doorways of heaven
seem to open wider
toward the end of the calendar year
as though a traffic light turns green or maybe
white
lights the tunnel.

~~~

Experience happens all the time.

Perspective
only when you give it truth-telling attention.

~~~

If you don't take responsibility for your actions,
you're really lying to yourself.

~~~

Being human isn't being perfect,
it's being real.

~~~

You can't get past ignorance
if you keep ignoring what you've done.

~~~

When you're tired
of hearing yourself tell your same story,
change is on the horizon.

~~~

Perspective takes some
of the bitter out of bittersweet.

~~~

The grist of life is ground finely
through humility and gratitude.

~~~

If you open a can of worms
use them to fish for something better.

~~~

It's easy to use
your outdated state of understanding
to judge someone.
Don't.

~~~

Healing
takes place in the open
which turns into strength
which turns into boldness.
Don't be afraid to talk about your troubles.

~~~

You don't need
to hold on to the question
if you have a relationship with the answer.

~~~

My volcano
is alive and well
never to become dormant yet no longer a danger.

~~~

Knowledge is not wisdom.
Strength is not power.
Discernment is the key, the tool,
to an honorable life.

~~~

Feelings
vs
talking about feelings
is a world of difference.

~~~

Running away from myself,
always seeing the fight in somebody else's eyes.
I didn't realize,
it was in **me** all along.

~~~

Navigate the path to inner trust
through wisdom and intuition.

~~~

Experience over time yields perspective.

~~~

Reconciling the past frees the present
and allows for greater possibilities in the future.

There's power in both the process and the result.

~~~

Experience provides the opportunity but
reflection promotes wisdom.

~~~

Wisdom
yields to grace.
Grace yields to wisdom.

A reciprocal, intimate relationship.

~~~

Integrate the experience of your greatness,
with grounded humility.

~~~

Realization is practiced
by taking something unreal or unformed
and making it real in this world.

~~~

Absolute truths aren't either.

~~~

"Truths"
are opinionated projections.

~~~

Nothing better than life experiences to humble
you and grow you up.

Often bittersweet,
often ironic
always grist
for the emotional and spiritual mills.

~~~

There's a big difference between
being self-conscious and self-aware.

~~~

Within tragedy there is peace,
within confusion there is stillness,
within fear there is love.

~~~

Life is not an endurance game,
but endure we do.

~~~

Gratitude is the language of God.
Feel it, speak it, show it
and you'll get back more to be grateful for.

~~~

I'm not wise just experienced.

~~~

You can't live your dreams until you wake up.

~~~

Depth of character and wisdom are hard won.

~~~

Grief is the tool
to integrate
the pain of the heart,
the choices of the mind and
the circumstances that befall us.

~~~

The purpose of *life* is one thing.
We don't get to define that.

The purpose of **our** lives is something quite
different.

~~~

Some say things didn't work out.

They worked out.

You were attached to a result and
you just didn't like the outcome.

~~~

I'll be me. You be you.
That's our nature. That's our destiny.

Anything else is a lie.

~~~

When there's a conflict between the mind and
emotions, emotions usually win.

Sometimes that's a good thing but not always.

~~~

Inner conflict
is a battle between the conscious and
subconscious.

Integration takes re-educating the subconscious
which is hard,
until it's not.

~~~

Wisdom is
the product of experience
and paying attention to consequences over time.

~~~

Be not swayed by the ripples
while another wave builds behind the rocks.

~~~

All love is self-love sometimes
inwardly directed other times outwardly.

~~~

The truth shall set you free
but it helps to have a good lawyer.

~~~

On your last trip
out the door
you're not taking anything in your pockets.

~~~

Life's too short
not to be who you are
but sometimes it takes awhile.

~~~

It's **No**
unless it's **Yes**.

~~~

Keep your eyes open,
let your intuition guide you,
follow your heart
but please
consult your brain.

~~~

Regret
can become inspiration
when mixed with missed opportunities.

~~~

Beauty, sadness and love
are the realm of the bittersweet.

~~~

Regret teaches us
not to miss opportunities
for love and growth.

~~~

Expectations and feelings
are dangerous bedfellows.

So are a lack of expectations.

~~~

If we're made
in the image of the creator
you'd better do some creating.

~~~

Some people strive for greatness
others have it thrust upon them.

~~~

On the flip side
of the ironies of life
are the serendipitous
synchronicities that abound.

~~~

Things aren't always
what they seem to be
or
what we fear them to be.

~~~

Some lessons
are cheaper than others.

And
for that matter,
some mistakes
are only worth making once.

~~~

Better to fall on your face
than to fall on your faith.

We all do one or the other, sometimes both.

~~~

Seeing clearly necessitates carrying the light.

~~~

If you don't embrace your shadow,
when it appears
you'll believe that's who you are.

~~~

Your "job" is to be the best you.
"Best" doesn't mean perfection, that's futility.

~~~

Perfection is an erroneous concept, not a lifestyle.

~~~

People agree
that a defect is not a good thing.
Understand that perfect isn't either.

~~~

I look back on my life and realize
I was stupid
but I don't care.
How I got here doesn't matter.
That I got here is all that matters.

~~~

Creativity is our essence, our gift, our mission.

~~~

If boredom sets in,
create something.
The process will make you come alive
even if the outcome doesn't.

~~~

Some things can go without saying
but still need to be said.

~~~

Throw open the blinds.
Let the light in.
Shine!

~~~

If you want to drink
from the stream of life
an open hand
yields more than a closed fist.

~~~

When you say "no" to something
the universe says
"oh, yes you will." *

*This isn't intended to mean
rejecting something unhealthy

~~~

Free your freedom.

~~~

You know what they say,
when you play with fire,
it's easier to light the way.

~~~

Music marks the decades,
each one gives us a new sound,
still we go back to the roots of our youth.

~~~

Humility is soothed
by the sweetness of
self-forgiveness and compassion.

~~~

Gratitude
is my superpower.
Humility keeps it in check.

~~~

Trust and surrender
are intimate bedfellows.

~~~

Love seems to work.

~~~

It's good to be alive while you're alive.

Don't wait for the last minute.

~~~

I want to take in all the tastes of life
because the smells don't fill my belly.

~~~

In the buffet
of love
where shall I nibble first?

~~~

I'm tasting
less bitter in the sweet.

~~~

When life gives you lemonade
you don't even have to squeeze the lemons.

~~~

The empty page
is the universe
and you are the artist.

~~~

Life
is God's gift to you.

Let your life show your gratitude. Let your actions
and thoughts be the gift you give in return.

~~~

My life is surrounded by creative excellence.

~~~

Life is a miracle,
spending it with friends and family is a blessing.

~~~

We are walking miracles;
biochemical, energetic, divine miracles.

~~~

Knowing yourself is indeed
the gift of a lifetime.

~~~

You're not different. You're unique.
That's the difference.

~~~

Whoever shows up first
gets the prize
but you have to keep showing up.

~~~

Things of the dark are kept under cover until they
can be kept quiet no longer.

~~~

The pregnant pause during transitions
is lovely and unsettling
until presence speaks its peace.

~~~

Eternity
is in the present moment.
So is divinity.

~~~

Time is moving at vacation pace.

~~~

Being high
is like being young only with wisdom.

~~~

The sound
of someone's crying
has no accent,
but for that matter,
neither does laughter.

~~~

Be the willing servant of intuition
and the blessings of life will rain upon you.

~~~

Become part of the living miracle.

~~~

Love doesn't die but loss tears us apart.

~~~

May Grace ease your suffering.
May memories keep your love alive.

~~~

Grief
is the pain of love unshared
and life unlived.

~~~

Grief is emotional duct tape.
It holds us together when our heart is falling apart.

~~~

Grief,
the healing path to wholeness and
a life of deeper connection to self and others.

~~~

Death:
the graduation
when we accept our diploma
of inconceivable love.

~~~

Part Two

Irony of life

+++

Striving to be myself
is a conflict between
being the best I can be and
the cantankerous rebel child
who runs the show,
often teamed up with the inner adolescent.

Sometimes they're my inspiration,
sometimes my nemesis.

+++

In school
I learned of the Law of Gravity.

In life
I learned of the Law of Irony.

Both are ever present but they take turns
at which is more annoying.

+++

I closed the heavy metal door
which rang
with the clang
of my personal prison.
It locked with a sense of finality.

I didn't realize I was on the wrong side.
Trapped like an animal,
I built the walls, the bars, the moat.

Many tools
would have kept me out of that dreadful place,
but no, accepting suggestions wasn't my strong
suit.

My mother always said I was stubborn.

+++

I've got to get "it" right.
Sometimes I think I'm close and then I slip
the slippery slope back to the mundane
pablum of life.

+++

My secret desire is
to be a balanced, integrated human but
my teeter-totter nature
isn't balanced any more
than a seesaw is
when it sees more than it saw.

+++

We deny it,
we avoid it,
we don't prepare for it.

Death being the only certain thing
which we treat
with less dignity and respect
than the illusory Santa Claus.

+++

From the moment
sperm and ovum unite,
division and unity become our rhythmic pattern.
How we blend them
becomes our life's path.

+++

It's a dangerous practice to be a hypocrite
but it seems we all are,
often in subtle ways even to ourselves.

+++

The benefit of aging is
you see a lot and you learn a lot.

The downside of aging is
you see a lot and lose a lot.

Still, I prefer it.

+++

The moments I want
to last forever
presuppose a forever,
simultaneously denying the present.

+++

Choices made during the course of life
don't early reveal
they are indeed,
life choices.

+++

The longer I live,
the more I see,
the more I realize
the less I know
and the less I know why we're here
and why we do anything.

It's not nihilistic, it's freeing.

+++

Living Life in Two Parts

I need to live my life so I don't have to hide from
my ex-anything.

&

I need to live my life
so I don't have to hide myself, from myself.

+++

Are coniferous trees God's way of saying
"I'm sorry about winter?"

+++

I look at the mountains and
see their majesty.

When I'm in the mountains
I can't see more
than the trees which surround me.

Distance can offer beautiful perspective.

+++

Is Death the end
or another beginning?

Maybe "life" is
the halftime entertainment.

Honestly,
we don't know
so we make up stories.

We can stop arguing and fretting about who has
the best story.
We'll find out,
unless we won't.

It shouldn't change our behavior in the meantime.

+++

Wisdom of life

~~~

Humility
is learned through experience
when consequences are integrated over time
by reflecting with an open mind.

~~~

We train ourselves
with the words that were programmed into us
and the ones we now recite.

Replace them, if need be.
Use them kindly toward yourself and others.
Include lots of love, self-acceptance, forgiveness
and compassion.

~~~

Everything is about Waking Up:
coffee, alcohol, art, relationships...

If you don't think that's true
you have some painful lessons ahead.

~~~

There's no Personal healing
without addressing your family.

There's no National healing
without addressing genocide and slavery.

There is no Gender healing
without addressing the patriarchy.

There is no Global healing
without addressing the monetary system.

Look to the core. Anything else
is a superficial step which,
may inform
but
won't make a radical change.

~~~

The one job we have is to become ourselves.
Ironic, isn't it?

We try to be us and the trying takes us away.

Surrender to your quirks,
surrender to self-compassion,
surrender to self-love.

Therein lies the secret of self-discovery.

Become your integrated, accepted self.

That's when true living begins.

~~~

The Cycle of Life
Chaos
Control
Order
Chaos
Surrender
Integration
Surrender

~~~

Steps to Self-Realization

Self-Knowledge: observing your behavior.

Self-Understanding: knowing your motives.

Self-Acceptance: utilizing forgiveness.

Self-Confidence: through inspiration to act.

Self-Esteem: feeling your innate worth.

Self-Actualization: bringing your wholeness
to this world.

Self-Realization: making your being real
in the spiritual world.

~~~

Fear believes
it's all about me.

Projection and idealization believe
it's all about you.

Love knows
it's all about us.

~~~

Accomplishments are not what I thought.

I've done and acquired many things,
but they all pale in comparison
once I finally became myself.

~~~

Wisdom, the tool of tools:
knowing when to act,
when to watch and
when to strike with clarity
to exact the effect
not just desired but appropriate and needed.

This is life,
living with intuition, integrity and intelligence.

~~~

If you never
test your boundaries or press your limits,
you'll spend your life living in a box
that doesn't exist.

~~~

I was trained
to contain myself,
to constrain myself,
even stifle myself,
but fortunately
life has taught me better.

~~~

Warm Up for the Apocalypse

Zombie movies
gave us the preview.
Covid-19 was the pop quiz.
How will we behave
when the 4 horseman arrive?

~~~

Open your heart before you open your eyes,
otherwise you'll see through someone else's.

~~~

It's hard to imagine
we and the universe are one
yet that understanding
is exactly what we need to course correct
humanity.

~~~

Fear constructs walls
for self-protection.
Idealization seduces across boundaries.
Love uses integrity for healthy interaction.

~~~

The trip to the candy store is a sweet reward
after dining on savory foods.

It is dangerous however
to make a diet of candy no matter how sweet.

~~~

It takes
vulnerability and forgiveness
to live in goodness,
otherwise it's a shitshow
waiting for the curtain to rise.

~~~

What's behind your need
to assign spiritual meaning to an experience?

A dire hope that life makes sense?
A need to feel belonging
in a disconnected society?
If nothing else, it's a career path for philosophers,
scientists and artists.

~~~

If you want to understand the universe
you have to embrace paradox.

If you want to understand humanity
you have to have compassion.

If you want to understand yourself
you have to own your darkness.

~~~

There's personal time and there's God's time.

Confusing the two
leads to different conclusions; one logistical or
emotional and the other divine.

~~~

God is
the conscious creative vibration from which the
worlds were vibrated into existence.

We're sustained by that vibration, which is felt as
unconditional love.

~~~

Rocks, bark, cones, clouds, roots and
plants of many shapes and textures
tell me what I've suspected for so long.

Our creator is a show off.

~~~

If I were a God
I'd make miracles
sing through the breeze and
dance on the waves.
Subtlety my nature.

~~~

We get stronger over time through our
experiences. Life brings new ways
of stretching us open. They're not always easy but
they make us able to relate to others with more
compassion.

~~~

While thinking can help provide perspective
and perspective can influence feelings,
feelings come and go as they please.

~~~

Distractions and avoidance are still
you making a choice.

~~~

Caring attention is my gift of giving.
I can't control how or even if it's received.
I do know when it's received in the spirit
intended, it's golden.

~~~

I appreciate you loving me,
knowing what I know about myself.

~~~

Be forgiving and compassionate
with yourself and others.

~~~

www.ingramcontent.com/pod-product-compliance
Lightning Source LLC
Chambersburg PA
CBHW070459050426
42449CB00012B/3043